Perspectives
Natural Wonders of the World
How Do We Protect Them?

Series Consultant: Linda Hoyt

Flying Start
to Literacy®

Contents

Introduction 4

Exploring natural wonders 6

Striking a balance 8

The roof of the world 12

Real vs. replica 16

Uluru – to climb or not to climb? 20

What is your opinion?:
How to write a persuasive argument 24

How can we protect the natural wonders of the world?

Throughout the world there are many natural wonders that millions of people visit each year. Damage and even destruction of these amazing places has often been the result of too many tourists.

However, tourism is a massive industry worldwide. It could even help to protect habitats and the animals living in them. The balance between protecting natural environments and tourism is a tricky one.

Should tourists be allowed to visit places of natural wonder?

How can we make sure that natural habitats are suitably protected to allow future generations to see them?

Where does the balance lie?

Exploring natural wonders

Most adventurers and explorers appreciate the natural beauty the earth has to offer and they want to protect it for future generations. They live by the explorers' code shown here.

What do you think? Is it okay to collect a fossil from a beach? Does it matter if you leave a piece of trash at a park? Or do you, too, agree with this code?

How does the code protect our natural wonders?

Take nothing but photos.

Leave nothing but footprints.

Kill nothing but time.

Striking a balance

In this article, Jennifer Mason explains how the National Park Service in the United States balances preserving natural wilderness areas, while allowing public access.
Do we need rules, and why?

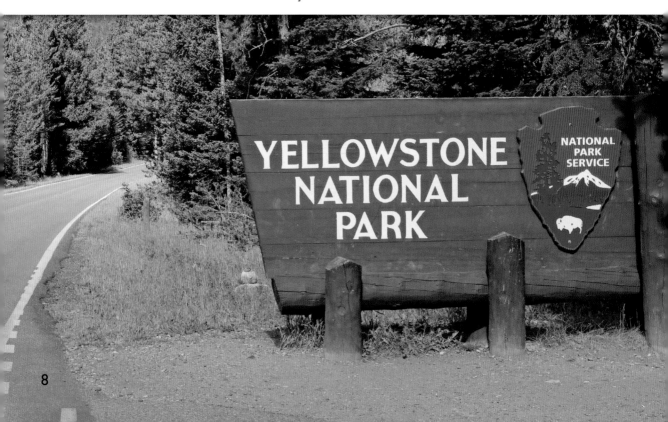

One day not long ago

Old Faithful steams and fizzes. Soon, the geyser will erupt into the sky with a giant spear of water! Park Ranger Valerie Gohlke waits with the thousands of visitors who travelled to Yellowstone National Park to witness the spectacle. A couple approaches Gohlke with a series of questions: Can they get married in front of Old Faithful? How much does it cost to rent the geyser? Could she recommend where to hang fresh flower garlands?

Gohlke patiently answers each of their questions. No one can rent the geyser, she explains. It is a wonder for the public to enjoy. When she says that absolutely no flowers may be brought into the park, the couple looks upset. Before she can explain how invasive flower species can destroy the local natural habitat, the geyser surges.

The Old Faithful geyser in Yellowstone National Park in the USA

Rules protect

These days, Gohlke is a park ranger at Carlsbad Caverns National Park in New Mexico in the United States. Like every national park, Carlsbad has its own special "wow" factor – more than 100 known limestone caves that were carved by sulfuric acid millions of years ago. Inside Carlsbad, visitors marvel at the range of speleothems – cave formations from mineral deposits that resemble ribbons, fangs and even popcorn.

At Carlsbad, balancing visitor use with park protection is extremely difficult. Natural oils on a person's hands can prevent the dripping water from depositing more minerals. One human touch can kill the fragile cave ecosystem and impact thousands of years of growth. The caves are also home to tens of thousands of hibernating bats, which can become sick if a fungal disease is introduced. Park rangers

make sure the soles of visitors' shoes are decontaminated before people enter the caverns.

According to Gohlke, park rangers "want everyone to have a fabulous experience and fall head over heels in love with the national parks. But the reality is, we're going to frustrate people with our rules." And just like the couple at Yellowstone, some people don't understand or like the restrictions.

As Gohlke says, "The parks were not created to just lock the gates and not let anyone in." Allowing people to see up close the natural wonders that exist in the United States helps gain support for the National Park Service's mission. So what's a ranger to do?

The King's Chamber in the lowest part of the Carlsbad Caverns, New Mexico, USA

The roof of the world

Each year, tens of thousands of tourists flock to Sagarmatha National Park in Nepal and trek up to the Mount Everest base camp. Their mission is to conquer Everest and reach the top. In this article, Stephen James O'Meara describes the risks and obstacles.

With so many people trying to conquer Everest, who protects this heritage-listed natural wonder? Should people be allowed to climb Mount Everest?

Mount Everest lies in the eastern Himalaya, the world's greatest mountain chain. The Himalaya stretch about 2400 kilometres east to west along the border of Nepal and Tibet.

Mount Everest, lying on Nepal's border with China, has drawn the bravest of souls. Standing a dizzying 8848 metres tall, the height at which many commercial airliners fly, Mount Everest is the pinnacle of the earth's surface. The summit's extreme environment threatens the life of anyone who attempts the two-month journey to the top. The frigid subzero temperatures, the sudden storms with 160-kilometre-per-hour winds and the thin air (containing only one-third of the oxygen we breathe at sea level) are obstacles that only the hardiest of humans can endure.

Then there are the physical traumas that attack at extreme altitude: snow blindness, frostbite, cuts that won't heal, pneumonia and ribs that fracture from coughing. And still the would-be conquerors try. Humans often speak of their accomplishments as conquests. In the case of Mount Everest, the word "conquer" seems much too bold.

Ask yourself these questions: Does anyone ever really conquer Everest? Can a human endure the summit's conditions for more than a few moments without the help of technology?

Today's climbers use an arsenal of equipment: oxygen canisters and masks; clothing with a polypropylene-lined inner layer for wicking sweat away from the body, a medium layer for insulation and an outer layer of waterproof Gore-Tex; ultraviolet-safe sunglasses; plastic boots with warm inner linings; crampons; ice axes; and strong, lightweight ropes and harnesses. In fact, anyone who can pay $65,000 (no refunds) can attempt to climb the mountain.

Some adventure travel companies run advertisements boasting trips with a 100 per cent chance of success. But this is folly. Only about one in seven climbers ever makes it to the top, and 275 people to date have died trying, including 22 people who died when an earthquake hit Nepal in April 2015. In fact, 2015 was the first year in 41 years that no climbers reached the summit. In time, humans will learn that Mount Everest is not a playground.

A human on Everest is like an ant clinging to an elephant's head – both are likely to be effortlessly crushed or brushed off at any moment. Can we ever conquer Everest? Has the ant on the elephant's head conquered its host?

Trekkers on the Everest trail

Real vs. replica

The Lascaux Cave system in France contains prehistoric rock paintings and, of course, everyone wanted to see them. But when scientists realised that moisture from people's breath was damaging these paintings, the caves were closed to the public. Today, people can visit a replica of these caves.

In this article, Claire Halliday discusses this situation. Is it okay to create a replica for people to visit if it preserves the original? How important is it to know that what you are seeing is real?

The discovery of the Lascaux Cave

The story goes that on 8 September 1940, a little black and white dog, named Robot, chased a rabbit down a hole near the village of Montignac in France. The dog's owner, Marcel Ravidat, 18, and three of his friends, got the dog back but returned a few days later to explore what they thought might be an underground cave.

What they found, with only the flickering light of their oil lamp to guide their way across the rocks, was a grotto – and incredible, colourful cave paintings.

Historic art

The paintings in the Lascaux Cave – where a layer of natural chalk had protected the surface from water – are the only ones whose original bright colours have not faded.

Experts estimate that the paintings are around 15,000 to 17,000 years old. The paintings mainly feature representations of different types of animals and are regarded as one of the finest examples of art from that time. The detailed paintings depict horses, red deer, stags, wild cattle, cats and what appear to be mythical creatures.

17

The impact of tourism

The Lascaux Cave was opened to the public in 1948. Unfortunately, the steady stream of visitors had a negative impact. Scientists believe that the visible deterioration of the paintings was caused by the bright lights used to display the artworks, as well as the added moisture from the breath of up to 100,000 visitors each year.

In 1963, the Lascaux Cave – listed as a UNESCO World Heritage Site – was closed as a tourist attraction to protect the 600 paintings and 1500 engravings from further damage.

Replicating art

In 1983, a replica of the Lascaux Cave, known as Lascaux II, was opened just 180 metres from the original site. Even though it is not the original artwork on display, the attraction has drawn more than 10 million visitors.

Another replica, Lascaux III, has been touring museums and galleries around the world. And in December 2016, Lascaux IV, which is an elaborate reproduction of the entire cave system, was opened to the public near where the original cave was found.

**A reproduction of the
original cave at Lascaux**

Recreating history

The idea of replicating art to preserve the original is
something that is becoming more common. In 2013, a
replica of King Tutankhamen's tomb opened in Egypt –
not far from the original historic tomb, which was discovered
by British archaeologist Howard Carter and his team in 1922,
after lying untouched for more than 3000 years.

The replica was created to help protect what was once
regarded as the best-preserved tomb found in the Valley
of the Kings. In the case of this tomb, until the original is
permanently closed to the public, tourists have a choice.

Will they choose to see something that helps protect our
history? Or will they choose the thrill of seeing something
they know is 3000 years old – even though they know that,
by seeing it, they are partly responsible for it not being
there in the future?

Which option would you choose?

Uluru – to climb or not to climb?

Imagine having a place that meant something very special to you. Now imagine hundreds of thousands of strangers coming to that special place to explore it, photograph it and even climb all over it.

That's what has been happening for decades at Uluru in the Northern Territory, says journalist Claire Halliday.

If you were the traditional owners of that special site, how would that make you feel?

According to the local indigenous Australians, the Anangu people, who are the traditional owners of Uluru, this world-famous rock formation is a sacred place that should be respected.

So, why do so many tourists still insist on their right to climb it – just for the experience of saying they've done it?

Although there is no official law that prevents tourists from climbing the impressive formation, signs and leaflets remind the site's 400,000 annual visitors that climbing Uluru shows a lack of respect for the spiritual significance of this important landmark. But even with this information so visible, it is estimated that around 38 per cent of all visitors to Uluru still climb the famous rock.

Would we allow visitors to act disrespectfully in one of our cathedrals?

People who support the "right" of visitors to climb Uluru, talk about the financial benefits of international tourism to the local economy. But local park guides say that there are lots of ways for visitors to enjoy Uluru without climbing it. The Uluru-Kata Tjuta National Park has many other attractions for tourists to enjoy, such as hiking, bike riding and guided tours. Local Anangu guides are also keen to educate visitors about desert culture.

Environmental damage is another reason why tourists should choose not to climb Uluru. While it may seem impossible to damage the huge sandstone rock formation, which stands 843 metres above sea level, erosion is already visible on the historic climbing route – a mark that is known as the "Scar of Uluru". The erosion has been caused by people climbing the rock.

When it comes to the debate about whether we should be able to climb Uluru, it's time to understand that preventing the damage that climbing causes Uluru is more important than the short thrill of a tourist attraction.

Archaeological evidence shows that indigenous Australians have lived in Central Australia for at least 30,000 years – proof of a rich history that deserves to be protected.

Prehistoric rock carvings at Uluru

What is your opinion?: How to write a persuasive argument

1. State your opinion

Think about the issues related to your topic. What is your opinion?

2. Research

Research the information you need to support your opinion.

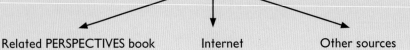

Related PERSPECTIVES book   Internet   Other sources

3. Make a plan

Introduction

How will you "hook" the reader?

State your opinion.

List reasons to support your opinion.

What persuasive devices will you use?

Reason 1
Support your reason with evidence and details.

Reason 2
Support your reason with evidence and details.

Reason 3
Support your reason with evidence and details.

Conclusion

Restate your opinion. Leave your reader with a strong message.

4. Publish

Publish your persuasive argument.

Use visuals to reinforce your opinion.